FOR ALL THE BILAN CHILDREN,
WITH LOVE X
JB

FOR DIDA, APARNA MAJUMDAR
CHAKRABARTI
NC

First published by Walker Books (UK) 2022 • Library of Congress Catalog Card Number 2022922950 • ISBN 978-1-5362-2501-3 • This book was typeset in Clarendon T and Gil Sans MT Schoolbook. The illustrations were done in mixed media.
Candlewick Press, 99 Dover Street, Somerville, Massachusetts 02144 • www.candlewick.com
Printed in Phu Ly City, Ha Nam, Vietnam • 23 24 25 26 27 28 VCI 10 9 8 7 6 5 4 3 2 1

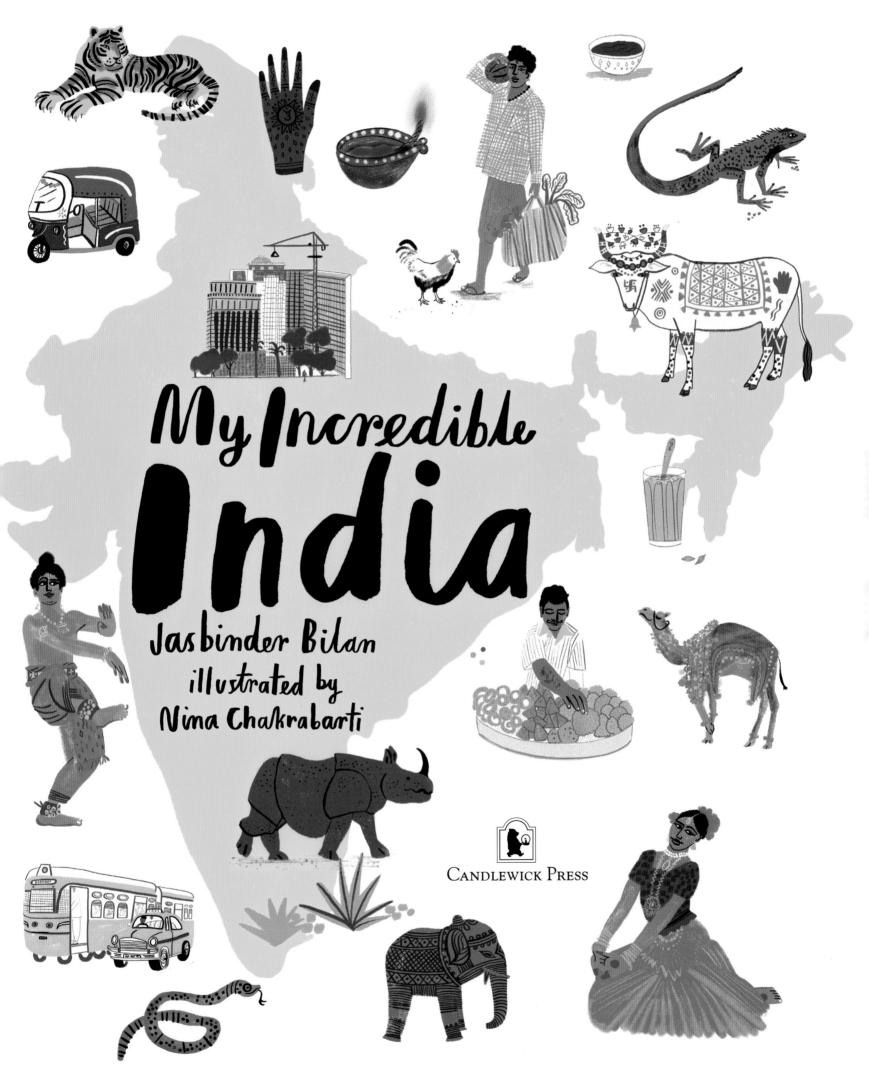

My Incredible India

Jasbinder Bilan

illustrated by
Nina Chakrabarti

CANDLEWICK PRESS

Jasbinder Bilan

I WAS BORN ON A FARM IN INDIA, close to the foothills of the Himalayas. As well as my family, I lived with a grumpy camel and a wild Indian monkey called Oma, who adopted us.

I was only one and a half years old when my family moved away, but whenever we gathered for big family dinners, everyone told stories of our life in India. There were stories of our beloved Oma and how she used to run off into the neem tree with my brother, sitting in the branches and rocking him to sleep. There were stories of the huge pans of popcorn that we used to cook on an outdoor fire under the starry skies. And there were stories of how, one day, we were going to have an adventure. We would travel back to India, hire a jeep, and head off on a trip around the country until finally we were on our farm again.

Writing this book about India has been like going on that journey: a sort of "welcome back." I found out so many things about India that I never knew before, and I can't wait to share them with you . . .

Nina Chakrabarti

I WAS BORN IN KOLKATA, one of the largest cities in India, to an English mother and a Bengali father. I loved growing up in such a huge place. The sidewalks were alive with bustling women wearing brightly colored saris and men with neat, oiled hair and fantastic mustaches. The hum of cars, trams, buses, and rickety rickshaws weaving their way around the city formed a soundtrack to my childhood.

Like Thara, whom you'll meet shortly, I was very close to my Indian grandmother. Her name was Aparna, but my sister and I called her Dida and spent long afternoons braiding and rebraiding her hair. She'd bat us away when it was time to cook, and I liked to watch her as she deftly added spices to a sizzling-hot pan. Years later when I moved to London, something about the city reminded me of Kolkata—perhaps because both cities are nestled into the mouths of majestic rivers, have inhabitants who speak many languages, and are made up of higgledy-piggledy streets with a mix of old and new buildings. I felt at home immediately.

 # Contents

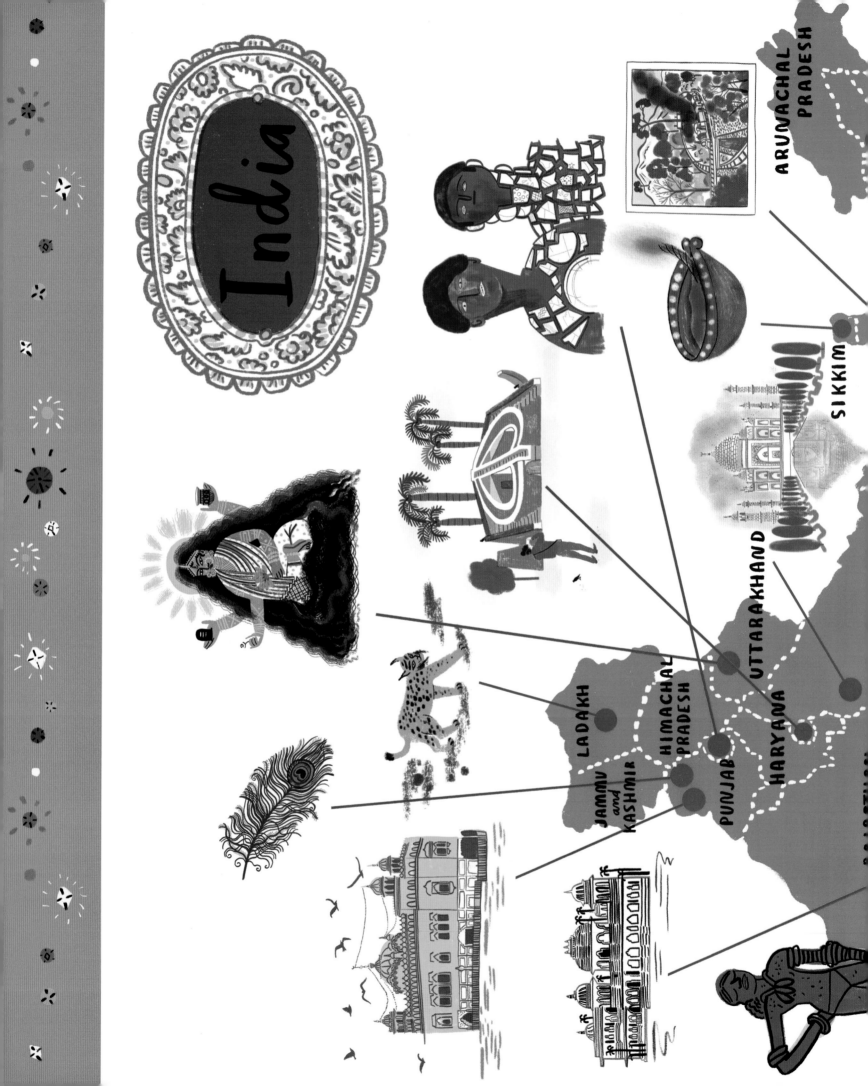

India

ARUNACHAL PRADESH

SIKKIM

UTTARAKHAND

LADAKH

HIMACHAL PRADESH

JAMMU and KASHMIR

PUNJAB

HARYANA

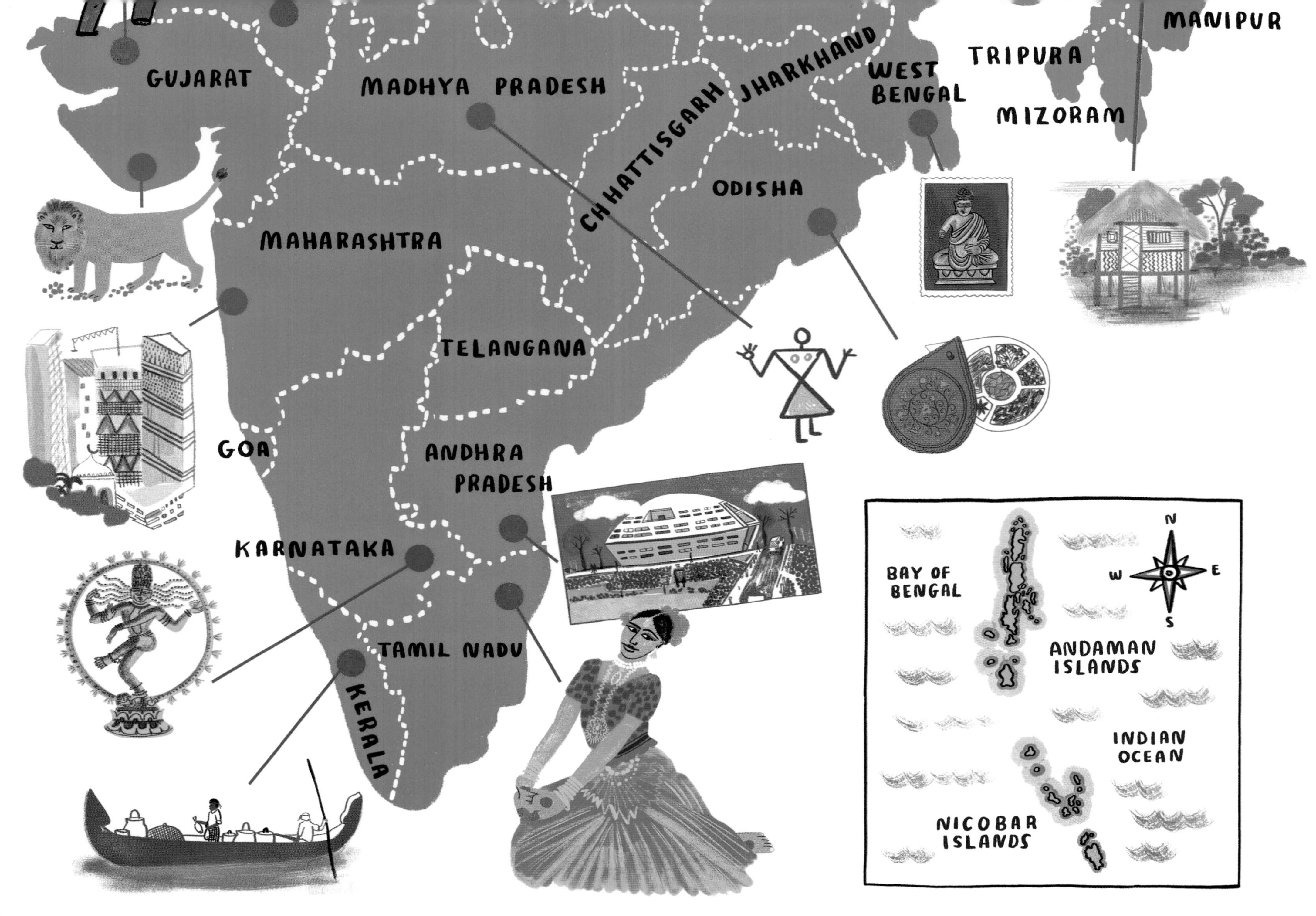

MANIPUR

TRIPURA

MIZORAM

WEST BENGAL

JHARKHAND

ODISHA

CHHATTISGARH

MADHYA PRADESH

MAHARASHTRA

TELANGANA

ANDHRA PRADESH

GUJARAT

GOA

KARNATAKA

TAMIL NADU

KERALA

N
E
W
S

ANDAMAN ISLANDS

INDIAN OCEAN

NICOBAR ISLANDS

BAY OF BENGAL

WELCOME to INDIA

INDIA IS JAM-PACKED WITH DIFFERENT LANDSCAPES. There are twenty-eight states and eight union territories, and each region is unique. There are scorching deserts, sacred rivers, and precious forests inhabited by endangered animals such as lions and tigers. To the north lie the snow-shrouded Himalayas, which run for around 1,500 miles (2,500 kilometers), and in the clear blue seas beyond India's shores, there are amazing islands with pristine beaches. It's a *huge* country, with a huge, welcoming heart.

The history of India stretches five thousand years into the past. It had some of the very first sophisticated cities in the world. If you go to India today, there are still ancient temples filled with sculptures and paintings, as well as wonderful historic palaces sitting like jewels in beautiful lakes.

There are also vibrant cities with modern skylines, such as New Delhi, Mumbai, and Kolkata. Like many cities around the world, India's cities are full of opposites: there are people who drive expensive cars and can spend all the money they like, and there are people who are forced to live on the streets. The buildings are home to both world-famous high-tech businesses and indoor bazaars and markets laden with handmade objects created using techniques that have been used for thousands of years.

One of the very special things about India is that it is a country of strong belief and faith. Hinduism, Buddhism, Sikhism, and Jainism were all born in India, and religions like Islam, Christianity, Zoroastrianism, the Baha'i Faith, and Judaism were brought to the country from elsewhere.

India now has the biggest population of Hindus in the entire world: over 900 million. Hinduism is one of the world's most ancient religions. Hindus believe in the circle of life and reincarnation, which means that after a person's death, their spirit does not disappear but passes into the body of another being and continues to live. This means that caring for wildlife is a big part of life for Hindus, because they never know who may have reincarnated in the creatures around them.

The most important texts in Hinduism are written in Sanskrit, India's ancient classical language. Sanskrit can be traced back to 1700−1200 BCE. Scholars think that all the European languages come from it; look how similar these words are: *mātr* (Sanskrit), *mater* (Latin), and *mother* (English).

To make sure that everyone understands each other, Hindi and English are the languages used all over India in newspapers and on the main TV stations. Here's how you say hello in a few of India's different languages:

HINDI
NAMASTE

PUNJABI
SAT SRI AKAL

TAMIL
VANAKKAM

URDU
AS-SALAAM ALAIKUM

ENGLISH
HI THERE!

About This Book

ALL THROUGH HER LIFE, Thara's nanijee has collected special objects from around India and kept them in a beautiful wooden trunk. Each object reminds her of a wonderful place she has visited.

This book will take you on a journey around India—you can read it all at once or dip into it when you feel like visiting a particular place. Every time you choose a page, it will be as though you are choosing an object from Nanijee's trunk yourself.

India is a land full of amazing things to discover. Things that will shake you up, take your breath away, and make you as curious as a monkey!

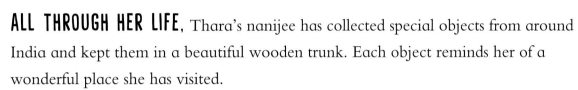

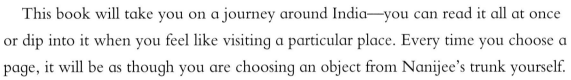

A JOURNEY AROUND INDIA

RIGHT AT THE TOP OF MY NANIJEE'S HOUSE, I have my own cozy room for sleepovers. My bed is layered high with a soft patterned rajai quilt, and Nanijee has hung an orange sari over it to make a canopy. In a corner of the room sits an old trunk made from sheesham wood, with beautiful carvings of elephants and tigers all over it.

Nanijee lived in India most of her life and has traveled all around the country. Wherever she went, she collected special objects as a reminder of each place—and all those objects are inside this wonderful trunk.

Friday nights are exciting nights: that's when I sleep over at Nanijee's. She makes me spiced milky chai sprinkled with cinnamon. I take a small sip and snuggle into the folds of her chunni. She smiles and creaks open the trunk. It smells sweet, like the heart of a tree.

She takes out one object and tells me all about it—which state it's from, why she loves it so much, and what makes it unique.

Each Friday night, I hurry up the stairs to my room, butterflies zipping through my stomach. I run my fingers along the carvings of the trunk and imagine all the things lying inside. All the things I'm going to see.

I wonder what Nanijee will show me tonight . . .

Uttarakhand
SOURCE OF THE RIVER GANGES

Nanijee reaches into the trunk and brings out a beautiful book. "I saw this at the Gangotri temple—and I knew you'd love it, Thara."

On the cover is a painting of the goddess Ganga. She wears a white dress, with a garland of red lotus flowers around her neck and bracelets of white jasmine on her wrists. Her long dark hair flows around her and blends into the white mountains behind.

She is the river Ganges: India's most sacred river.

"Snuggle in," Nanijee tells me, "and I'll tell you her story . . ."

THE STORY OF GANGA

In ancient times, the goddess Ganga watered the heavenly gardens. But her help was needed on earth, to wash away the ashes of the dead, so she came down from heaven. She was wildly powerful, cascading from the Himalayas in a fierce waterfall. To stop her from inadvertently destroying everything with her unbridled power, the god Shiva laid his heavy coiled hair in her way. She sank into his hair and began to flow majestically, gifting her waters to nourish the whole of India.

INDIA'S MOST IMPORTANT RIVER, THE HOLY GANGA (GANGES), STARTS ITS JOURNEY IN THE NORTHERN STATE OF UTTARAKHAND. IT BEGINS AT A PLACE HIGH IN THE HIMALAYAS CALLED GAUMUKH, WHICH FORMS PART OF THE GANGOTRI GLACIER.

GANGOTRI TEMPLE

The whitewashed Hindu temple at Gangotri is nestled in the Himalayas at a breathtaking altitude of 9,980 feet (3,042 meters). It's a magical place of myths and legends and is said to be where the goddess Ganga first came to earth.

Pilgrims cloaked in saffron cloth walk past the temple and into the mountains to reach the river's source at Gaumukh, which literally means "mouth of the cow." At Gaumukh, there is an ice cave where your breath puffs from your mouth; this is where the holy river is born, a milky stream bubbling from between the rocks.

Chandigarh

CHANDIGARH ROCK GARDEN

Nanijee passes me an envelope. I hold the worn paper gently and peek inside for the letter—but it's empty.

"The sculptures on this stamp are from the most incredible park," she tells me.

There are three figures dressed in bright rainbow-colored clothing.

"They look like toys, Nanijee," I say.

"They're made from things people have thrown away, and there are thousands of them—dotted between trees, perched on little hills, sitting beside the waterfalls . . ."

I stare again at the stamp and this little world, frozen in time.

SECRET FOREST
Nek Chand started his rock garden in 1957, in a hidden-away forest, so nobody knew about it. The garden was his secret! And it was nearly twenty years before the gardens opened to the public, in 1976.

RECYCLED WATERFALLS
Nek Chand built up a hill that's 100 feet (30 meters) high, complete with waterfalls that flow with recycled rainwater. Sculptures of women holding pots, as if to collect the rainwater, stand in some of the plunge pools.

CHANDIGARH IS IN THE FAR NORTH OF INDIA. IT'S THE CAPITAL OF BOTH PUNJAB AND HARYANA. IT TAKES ITS NAME FROM CHANDI, THE GODDESS OF POWER, AND *GARH*, WHICH MEANS FORT.

NEK CHAND

On the edge of the city of Chandigarh, deep in the forest, a man named Nek Chand decided to create a sculpture garden using waste material from the city. He wasn't a professional artist, just someone who loved being creative. During the day he worked as a road inspector, and after work he would come to the forest and let his imagination go wild! Many of the sculpted figures are covered in broken bits of ceramics. It's an enchanting place.

Nek Chand died in 2015, aged ninety. A rock at the entrance to the park celebrates his life.

ROCK GARDEN
A FANTASY CREATED BY NEK CHAND
DEDICATED TO THE SPIRIT OF CREATIVITY BY THE PEOPLE OF INDIA

DELHI

Nanijee brings out a small metal tuk-tuk. Its roof is painted bright red and it has three small wheels.

"You'd love Delhi so much, Thara. There are monkeys running around everywhere, and they're so cheeky, they might steal an ice cream right out of your hands!

"The best way to get around is on one of these tuk-tuks . . . but you have to watch out for the cows weaving through the blaring traffic."

I pull the tuk-tuk back and let it skid across the floor. "Coming through!"

Nanijee tells me all about Delhi at nighttime: about how she mingled with the crowds, sipping a lemon-sherbet drink as she went, and shopped at the late markets, all lit up by strings of lights.

"Delhi's got everything, Thara: beautiful old buildings, modern skyscrapers, and as much street food as you can eat!"

STARGAZING
If you want to find out about the stars and planets, head over to Jantar Mantar, an observatory built in 1724.

LIVING HISTORY
Old Delhi grew up around the famous Red Fort. When it was built, the decapitated bodies of prisoners were buried under the foundations—to bring good luck!

Every night visitors can watch a spectacular light and sound show at the fort. The whole building comes to life with storytelling. I wonder if any of the ghostly prisoners come out to play . . . and what stories they might tell!

KUSHTI

Kushti is an Indian martial art, with its own academy in the city. It's a mix of yoga and full-body contact, with very intense training. The monkey god, Hanuman, is its patron.

DELHI IS MADE UP OF TWO PARTS: OLD DELHI, WHICH IS THE ORIGINAL CITY, AND NEW DELHI, WHICH WAS DESIGNED BY EDWIN LUTYENS IN 1912 AND IS INDIA'S CAPITAL.

MUGHAL CITY

Old Delhi was founded by the Mughal emperor Shah Jahan in 1648 and was originally named Shahjahanabad.

ANCIENT AND MODERN

New Delhi is an amazing mix of old and new—ancient temples sit beside shops, art galleries, and outdoor water parks!

A BIRD PARADISE

Keoladeo National Park, in Rajasthan, is a stop along the Central Asian Flyway, a flight path for migratory birds. In the warmth of the winter sun, its glistening shallow lake fills with beautiful birds, including pink-backed pelicans; painted storks, with their rose-tipped feathers; and black-headed ibises, dipping their sharp curled beaks into the blue water, hoping to catch a fish for a snack!

WILDLIFE

Did you know that India is bursting with wildlife? Deep in teak forests, hidden in grasslands, high in mountains, and under the surface of India's holy rivers, magnificent animals—elephants, tigers, monkeys, leopards, and even lions—are everywhere. And of course sacred doe-eyed cows can even be found meandering through traffic-filled cities.

There are more than a hundred national parks in India, where wardens and conservationists work hard to protect these animals, many of which are endangered. Corbett National Park was the first to open and is one of the places Bengal tigers are thriving. Their orange and black stripes are like human fingerprints—no two tigers have the same markings!

Not many people realize that, in addition to tigers, India is home to Asiatic lions, which are highly endangered. Although they once used to roam all over Asia, from Syria to eastern India, the Gir Forest, in Gujarat, is now the lions' only sanctuary.

LOOKING FOR LEOPARDS

In the emerald-green forests of the Satpura National Park live leopards, sloth bears, black bucks, and delicate chital deer, their brown backs spotted white as if with snowflakes.

TIGER SPOTTING

Riding in a boat through the mangrove swamps of the Sundarbans National Park, keep your eyes peeled for a Bengal tiger, India's national animal, cooling itself in the fresh waters of the Ganges delta.

ENDANGERED BUT PROTECTED

Smooth gray river dolphins glide through the waters of Kaziranga National Park. And on land, among the tall waving elephant grass, one-horned rhinos—brought back from near extinction—are thriving.

Uttar Pradesh

THE TAJ MAHAL

THE TAJ MAHAL IS IN THE ANCIENT CITY OF AGRA, IN THE NORTHEAST STATE OF UTTAR PRADESH. IT DATES BACK TO 1632, THE TIME OF THE MUGHAL EMPERORS, WHEN MANY BEAUTIFUL, RICHLY DECORATED BUILDINGS WERE BUILT THROUGHOUT INDIA.

Nanijee is holding the Taj Mahal—a tiny one, carved from pale marble. She lights a candle and tucks it inside, and the walls begin to glow.

"Is it a palace, Nanijee?" I ask, peering closer at the red flowers that circle and weave around the arches.

"It looks like a palace—but no, Thara. It's a memorial."

She places the Taj Mahal in my hands and begins another of her stories: "There once was an emperor who married a princess named Mumtaz Mahal."

(It sounds like the start of a fairy tale!)

"One sad, sad day," Nanijee continues, "the princess died. The emperor loved her so much that he wanted everyone to remember her.

"And so he gathered all the best artists in India . . . and *that's* how the Taj Mahal was built."

PERFECT PEACE

Bathed in rosy light, the Taj Mahal sits high above the Yamuna River. As dawn breaks, a black-necked stork flaps from the water, its broad wings splashing the silence.

The front of the Taj Mahal is decorated with inlaid precious gemstones forming twisting green stems dotted with vibrantly colored flowers, created using the ancient craft of pietra dura, which literally means "hard stones."

ARCHWAYS

The archways are covered with black marble writing from the Quran. The words describe paradise and give reassurance that Mumtaz Mahal's spirit is welcomed there.

MARBLE BEAUTY

The Taj Mahal is surrounded by lush gardens filled with the sweet scent of beautiful red roses. A long pool bordered by tall cypress trees reflects the building's facade. Inside the silent structure lie the tombs of Mumtaz Mahal and her husband, Shah Jahan. Every evening, the glowing sun spreads through the latticed jali windows, casting light patterns onto the tombs.

RABINDRANATH TAGORE

Tagore was one of India's most famous poets. He called the Taj Mahal "a teardrop on the cheek of eternity," because it is so beautiful and may last forever.

Madhya Pradesh

BHIMBETKA CAVE PAINTINGS

THE BHIMBETKA CAVES, IN THE CENTRAL STATE OF MADHYA PRADESH, CONTAIN PREHISTORIC PAINTINGS THAT ARE THOUGHT TO BE UP TO TEN THOUSAND YEARS OLD.

Nanijee hands me a sketchbook, small enough to fit inside my pocket.

"What are all these stick people?" I ask as I open it up.

Nanijee tells me that she copied them from the ancient paintings in the Bhimbetka caves.

"I used the same colors in my sketches as the Stone Age people did—except the paints came from my little paint set, and theirs came from crushed rock and plants."

"This one's got huge horns!" I say, studying her drawing of a water buffalo. "And this bear—you can see right inside his ribs."

I close my eyes and imagine I'm there—right in the dappled shade of the teak forests surrounding the caves.

What was that? Heavy thudding, pounding closer: something big, with loud hooves clattering on the dusty ground.

"Scary," I decide. "I'm glad I didn't live in the Stone Age!"

ANCIENT ART
The Bhimbetka site has more than 750 caves, 500 of which contain paintings. It's like a Stone Age art gallery. There are many styles of images, including outlines, silhouettes, and "X-ray" drawings, which show what the animals have been eating.

LOST AND FOUND

The caves lay undiscovered for years until, in 1957, Indian archaeologist Dr. Vishnu Wakankar spotted them while traveling on a train and began to excavate the site.

ZOO ROCK

One of the caves is called Zoo Rock, because its paintings show hundreds of animals such as deer, chickens, and water buffalo. In the middle is an elephant rider, now called a mahout, who's trying to get past—it's a bit like an ancient traffic jam!

ANIMAL NEIGHBORS

In the majestic forest outside the Bhimbetka caves, black-faced langur monkeys and bright-green lizards spend their days scrambling over rocks.

Sikkim

CELEBRATING DIWALI

Nanijee shows me a pretty diya light. It's made of clay and painted bright green, with small pieces of sparkling glass around the rim.

"The family I stayed with in Yuksom in the Himalayas gave it to me when we celebrated Diwali together. There was no moon that night, and even though it was only October, being high in the mountains meant it was a bit chilly."

"And did you light it?"

"Oh, yes. We put lights all around the paths outside, sipped chai, and ate barfi layered with silver leaf."

"I want some barfi, too!" I jump under the covers. "Can we light your diya now?"

She sets the glowing light on the windowsill and cuddles in next to me. I feel a tingle, and know she's about to tell me a story . . .

WHAT'S IN A NAME?
The name Diwali comes from the Sanskrit word *deepavali*, which means a row of lights.

SWEET TREATS
Diwali is a time for family to get together, relax, and enjoy a party atmosphere with lots of food, especially sweet treats such as chirote, a light-as-air flaky pastry, and karanji, small pockets of rich pastry stuffed with grated coconut, sugar, cardamom, poppy seeds, and nuts.

Beautiful rangoli patterns are everywhere during Diwali. Working with colored flour, rice, and flower petals, you can let your imagination go wild!

22

RAMA AND SITA: THE DIWALI STORY

Prince Rama was the son of a great king. He should have become king himself, but his evil stepmother wanted her own son to inherit the throne. So she persuaded Rama's father to banish his dear son and daughter-in-law, Sita, from the kingdom.

Rama and Sita didn't realize, until it was too late, that the forest where they had made their home for fourteen years was full of demons. And one day, Ravana, the ten-headed demon king, decided to kidnap Sita.

After much fighting, Rama and his brother Lakshmana, with help from the monkey god Hanuman, finally rescued Sita—who had cleverly dropped her jewels to make a trail all the way to the island of Lanka, where she was imprisoned.

Rama, Lakshmana, and Sita made their way home on a moonless night guided by flickering diya lights that the people of the kingdom had laid along the path. This gesture showed that goodness had won over evil.

DIWALI IS CELEBRATED ALL OVER INDIA BY HINDUS, SIKHS, AND JAINS IN OCTOBER OR NOVEMBER. THE EXACT DATE CHANGES DEPENDING ON THE CYCLE OF THE MOON.

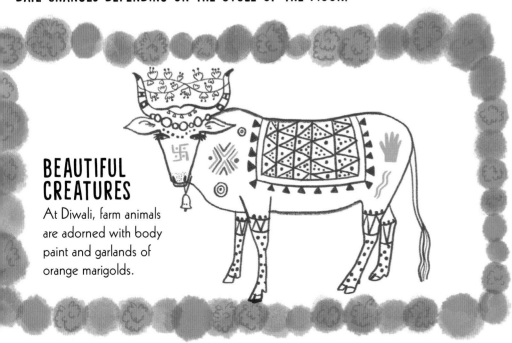

BEAUTIFUL CREATURES

At Diwali, farm animals are adorned with body paint and garlands of orange marigolds.

THE BIRTH OF MAHAVIRA

The birth of Mahavira is celebrated by Jains in late March or early April. His statue is bathed in liquid offerings such as milk and decorated with flowers, then carried through the streets.

RELIGIOUS FESTIVALS

India is a country with a long history of religious beliefs and a whole kaleidoscope of different faiths: Hinduism, Islam, Sikhism, Buddhism, Jainism, and other faiths all sit side by side.

Each of these religions is based around stories: stories of the many gods and goddesses of Hinduism; stories from the Islamic holy book, the Quran; stories of the Sikh gurus; stories of the Buddha; and stories of the Jain teacher Mahavira.

Each faith also has its own special festivals, and with so many religions in one country, the wonderful thing is that there's always a celebration to be had. And celebrations mean food, music, laughter, and fun. They're about getting together with family and friends and giving thanks for all of the good things in your life.

Festivals are also an opportunity to go on a trip or pilgrimage, and lots of people travel huge distances so they can join with groups to carry out rituals like bathing in the rivers. The holy river Ganga (Ganges) is worshipped by people of many faiths across India, including Hindus and Sikhs. Ganga is treated as a goddess, so submerging yourself in the river's waters during a festival is thought to bring lots of luck for the coming year.

LOSAR

Buddhists celebrate the New Year with the festival of Losar. It's a feast for the eyes, with everyone dressing up, wearing colorful masks, and dancing in the streets.

PUSHKAR CAMEL FAIR

The Pushkar Camel Fair takes place at the edge of the golden Rajasthani desert and lasts for seven days. It celebrates the festival of Kartik Purnima. The camels arrive bejeweled and decorated in colorful tassels and pom-poms to parade about the magical tented setting. In the light of the full moon, pilgrims submerge themselves in Pushkar Lake and, palms together, wish for blessings from the gods.

HOLI

Holi is the Hindu festival of color, and you'd better watch out, because it gets messy! It takes place in spring and is all about nature returning to color. You get to throw fistfuls of powder in a rainbow of hues at whoever you like— your mom, your dad, even teachers! People light bonfires to celebrate the god Vishnu's victory over the demon goddess Holika.

KUMBH MELA

One of the biggest Hindu festivals is Kumbh Mela, in Allahabad, where followers of Lord Shiva, dressed in dhotis and garlands of gold marigolds, gather to bathe where three holy rivers meet at Sangam. How many people do you think attended Kumbh 2019? Get ready . . . 220 MILLION! It's so huge, it can be seen from outer space!

GURPURAB

Guru Nanak Gurpurab, celebrated mostly in northern India, is one of the most important Sikh festivals. The dark November nights are brought to life with firecrackers, glowing lights, and shared palmfuls of delicious karah prasad: a sweet offering blessed by priests and eaten in blissful prayer.

EID AL-FITR

Eid al-Fitr is an Islamic celebration that marks the end of the dawn-to-dusk fasting of Ramadan. All over India, Muslims attend Eid prayers at mosques, donate to charity, and visit friends and family to share food and gifts.

MAJULI ISLAND

Nanijee hands me a shiny pod. It's a deep brown color, and when I shake it, it makes a rattling sound.

"I brought this back from beautiful Majuli Island," says Nanijee. "Can you hear the seeds inside?"

Nanijee then tells me about Jadav Payeng, the Forest Man of India. With seeds just like these, he created a new forest, all by himself!

"If we planted them," says Nanijee, "the seeds would turn into a silk tree, with feathery leaves and pink flowers as fluffy as cotton candy." Her face looks peaceful. "All you can hear on the island is the sound of wading birds splashing the clear waters. And there's so much wildlife—it felt like I was on safari as we walked through Jadav's forest, rustling with the footsteps of all the animals that live there."

"I want to go," I say, giving the pod another shake. "Can we plant the seeds first thing tomorrow?"

Every year, the monsoon brings heavy rain to Majuli. The water is so fierce and strong that the Brahmaputra River floods; it has sometimes swept away whole villages. But the roots of Jadav's trees hold the riverbanks together and protect the villagers.

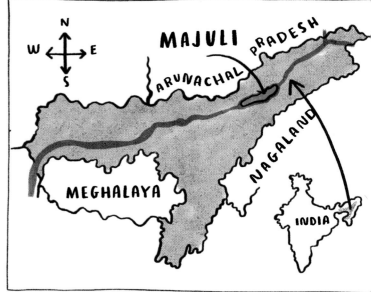

26

JADAV PAYENG

When he was sixteen, Majuli islander Jadav "Molai" Payeng found hundreds of dead snakes along the shores of the river. Without shade, they were being roasted alive by the strong sun! So he began to plant trees—bamboo at first, as it was the only plant that could grow in the sand, and then silk trees as the vegetation began to spread away from the river. Forty years later, he has created a beautiful forest, named Molai Forest in his honor.

FOREST BABIES

Now the Molai Forest is home to some amazing wildlife such as rhinos and wild boars. And—cute alert!—in 2012, the first tiger cubs to be born there arrived!

TALL CRANES

Flocks of sarus cranes like to wade in the river. They have white feathers tipped in black, long red legs, and a red face—and make a trumpeting sound so loud it will make you jump. They're the world's tallest flying birds!

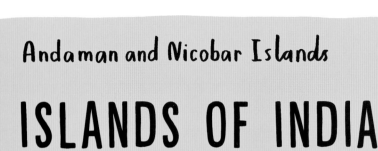

Andaman and Nicobar Islands

ISLANDS OF INDIA

LIKE AN EMERALD NECKLACE, THE ANDAMAN AND NICOBAR ISLANDS ARE SCATTERED ACROSS THE BLUEST WATERS OF THE BAY OF BENGAL.

I can't believe my eyes when Nanijee leans into the trunk and brings out a coconut!

"Can we split it open?" I ask her, running my palm along the rough hairy surface, imagining the yummy white flesh inside.

"Of course we can!" Nanijee smiles. "But don't you want to hear where it comes from?" And then, when I nod, she says, "Think of an island where tall coconut palms grow, all along sugar-white beaches."

I close my eyes, listen to her words, and slowly I can see it all: the beaches and the turquoise water brimming with dolphins and bright coral . . .

And best of all, I can see the baby sea turtles that Nanijee saw scampering over the sand, heading out into the dark sea at night as the stars twinkle above.

ANDAMAN ISLANDERS
Among the Andaman islanders, there are four distinct Indigenous peoples: the Great Andamanese, Onge, Jarawa, and Sentinelese.

TURTLE

SEA COW

WHITE-BELLIED SEA EAGLE

EAGLE-EYED
Majestic white-bellied sea eagles perch on the islands' forested cliffs, eyeing unsuspecting fish, turtles, and sea snakes in the green waters below.

THE ISLANDS
The Andaman and Nicobar Islands comprise about six hundred small islands, though only thirty-eight have people living on them. The islands are in fact the submerged peaks of the Arakan mountain range. It's an area known for earthquakes, which can sometimes cause tsunamis that bring terrible destruction.

BAY OF BENGAL

N
W   E
S

ANDAMAN ISLANDS

INDIAN OCEAN

NICOBAR ISLANDS

SEA SNAKE

MOORISH IDOL

GENTLE GIANTS
The docile dugong, or sea cow, is the islands' state animal and feeds on seagrass that grows in coastal waters.

THE QUEEN OF THE HILLS

Next out of the trunk is a train ticket. There's small writing all over it: at the top it says HAPPY JOURNEY, and in the center there's a wheel symbol.

शुभ यात्रा HAPPY JOURNEY
NFR TICKET चिकट नं. TICKET NO. 3626 4229
NORTHERN RAILWAY
DARJEELING PLATFORM 2
KURSEONG PLATFORM
1 Person (s)
Rs.84.00—

"See here," says Nanijee, showing me the edge of the ticket. "NORTHERN RAILWAY. Riding this little train is like going on a journey into the past. It's been taking passengers into the Himalayas for a very long time."

"What was it like?" I ask her.

"I remember watching the crew getting the engine ready, polishing the old brass dials—and the steam from the train puffing into the cold air." Nanijee smiles. "They even offered me a hot cup of chai. And then we were off, away into the mountains. You would have loved the noise: *choo-choo-choooo . . .*"

"*Choo-choo-choooo!*" I join in—and we chuff along together.

TAKING THE TRAIN
You can get almost anywhere in India by train. Most people travel crammed into third-class cars, as only the richest can afford the air-conditioned luxury of first class, with meals brought to their seats.

TIME FOR TEA
In India there's always time for chai, or black tea. Tea bushes like rain, and the hills of the Himalayas have a long history of growing tea, its deep-green leaves dried to make the perfect cup. India is the world's top tea producer.

DARJEELING HIMALAYAN RAILWAY

Painted in ornate gold and red, the inside of this train is as pretty as the landscape outside the window.

At some points of the journey, the road is right beside the train and cars pass alongside. The track even goes through the bazaar at Kurseong, so you can reach out to the colorful stalls and do some shopping if you like!

Sometimes the little train has to almost lean across the steep hills, balancing in midair. One of the tightest curves is called Agony Loop, because everyone has to hold their breath in agony until the train has safely rounded the sharp bend!

West Bengal
KOLKATA ARTS AND ARTISTS

Nanijee lays out a long line of postcards, including one of a shining bronze statue.

"When I went to Kolkata, the place I was really excited about visiting was the Indian Museum. They had so many paintings and beautiful statues of the Buddha—and this was my favorite. I sat in the courtyard afterward, watching birds swooping down to drink at the pool, thinking about the art I'd seen."

India has so many brilliant artists, Nanijee tells me. There was a group of painters who formed the Bengal School, which was very famous all over the world and started in Kolkata.

Nanijee shows me another postcard. "This painting is by Abanindranath Tagore."

"Is that the Buddha, too?"

"Yes, clever you, it is. It's called *Buddha and Sujata*."

"I love the colors on this painting, Nanijee. It looks so peaceful."

"Kolkata is such a buzzing city, Thara, with so much to do. You can see groundbreaking theater or browse fancy shopping malls. And the flower market is heavenly. I remember the clouds of jasmine scent wrapping themselves around me as I chose flowers to take to the temple."

I take a deep breath, imagining the perfume floating up to my nose.

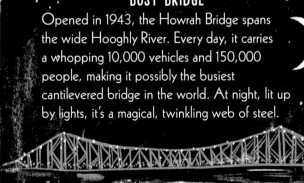

BUSY BRIDGE
Opened in 1943, the Howrah Bridge spans the wide Hooghly River. Every day, it carries a whopping 10,000 vehicles and 150,000 people, making it possibly the busiest cantilevered bridge in the world. At night, lit up by lights, it's a magical, twinkling web of steel.

GREEN SPACE

The Maidan, a huge green space right in the center of the city, is the place to hang out with your friends, go for a cool evening walk with family, or play a game of soccer.

SPORTING CITY

If you like sports, then Kolkata is perfect: Eden Gardens is the third largest cricket stadium in the world. And get your sugar cubes ready for the ponies at the world's oldest polo club, the Calcutta Club!

FROM A TO B

Zip around the city on the yellow trams or hop in one of the old-fashioned Ambassador taxis.

FAMOUS ARTISTS

There are many famous artists from the Bengal School, an art movement from the early 1900s based in Kolkata, including Abanindranath and Gaganendranath Tagore (nephews of the Nobel Prize–winning poet and philosopher Rabindranath Tagore), Nandalal Bose, and Jamini Roy. Art is a big part of Indian life; modern Indian artists include Rekha Rodwittiya and Latika Katt.

ABANINDRANATH AND GAGANENDRANATH TAGORE

JAMINI ROY

BHUBANESWAR SPICE MARKET

Nanijee picks out a wooden spice box. The lid is carved with flowers, and when you swing it to the side, you can see six compartments filled with fragrant spices.

"I bought it from a market in Bhubaneswar," says Nanijee, lifting the box so I can smell the spices. "Some families pass their masala dabbas on through the generations. This one was used in a kitchen for a long time."

There's a star-shaped spice in one of the sections and I lift it to my nose.

"That's star anise," says Nanijee. She points to each compartment and shows me the spices: cardamom, yellow turmeric, black pepper, cloves, and cumin.

"What are we going to make with them?" I ask.

"How about the Bhubaneswar version of gupchup?"

It already smells like a spice market—I can't wait!

CARDAMOM
Like bright-green jewels, cardamom pods grow at the base of the plant. The pods and seeds can be dried and ground; cardamom is added to tea to make chai, as well as to sweet dishes such as kheer. It's also often used as part of the masala, or spice mix, in savory dishes.

CITY OF TEMPLES
Bhubaneswar, which is also known as the city of temples, sits on the Mahanadi River close to the Bay of Bengal. It is hot and humid. Palm trees line its roads, and the river is filled with wildlife: crocodiles, rare dolphins, and thousands of nesting birds.

x x ♡ x x
Nanijee

to Thara
Elm Bank
Nottingham
UNITED KINGDOM

10¢ INDIA

BHUBANESWAR IS KNOWN FOR ITS SPICE GROWING. ACROSS INDIA, EACH REGION USES SPICES IN A UNIQUE WAY TO CREATE WONDERFULLY VARIED DISHES.

FOOD IN BHUBANESWAR

Bhubaneswar is famous for some delicious and unusual dishes, such as fried pumpkin flowers; dhal cooked with potato; plantains; and eggplant fried in a five-spice mix and topped with grated coconut. And food is often served on a huge banana leaf! If you have a sweet tooth, you will love chhena poda. Its name literally means "burnt cheese"; it's cooked with sugar, creamy cashew nuts, and fat raisins.

DABBAWALLAHS

Can you imagine your mom or dad sending your favorite hot lunch to school at midday? In Mumbai, an army of dabbawallahs zoom around the city on bikes, collecting lunch boxes called tiffin tins from homes and delivering them to hungry office workers.

FOOD

Food, glorious food—India has an obsession with it. And why not?

Food is very much the spice of life, and all over this wonderful country, it is celebrated and properly worshipped. Bowls of milk, fruit, and nuts are put before the gods in temples and shrines, asking for their blessing and as a way of giving thanks. And anyone can go to a Sikh gurdwara and enjoy a delicious langar meal for free: it's part of this religion to feed people.

In addition to food in home kitchens, you can eat just about anywhere and anytime you feel a grumble in your stomach. Each region has its own specialties using fresh local ingredients. In the south, many dishes are based around creamy coconuts, which grow on palm-fringed beaches, whereas in the north, recipes are flavored with tomatoes and served with flatbreads such as roti or naan cooked in clay ovens called tandoors.

It is thought that around a third of the country is vegetarian: around 500 million people. Cows are sacred in Hinduism, and killing cattle is illegal in the majority of Indian states. Because of this, you can eat the most incredibly imaginative, delicious vegetarian food in India.

FOOD ON THE GO

Food on the go is a big thing, and you just need to follow your nose to find the best street stall. Vast pans of hot oil crackle like fireworks every time a ladleful of pakora batter is dropped in before emerging golden—perfect with a dollop of tamarind chutney.

SWEETS

And then there are the sweets! Shops and stalls all have their own secret recipes for treats such as fudge-like barfi, brushed with a layer of edible silver leaf, and glowing yellow laddu, sugar-rich and made with chickpea flour.

DUMPLINGS

In the mountainous state of Arunachal Pradesh, the dishes are a fusion of Chinese and Indian influence, including fish momos (a sort of delicious steamed dumpling), creamy milk from long-haired yaks, and rice cleverly cooked in a bamboo tube.

KALAKSHETRA DANCE ACADEMY

Jingle! Jangle!

Nanijee is shaking a pair of ankle bracelets: they're made of yellow cotton, with three rows of bells sewn onto the fabric.

"I hope they fit," she says, tying them around my ankles. "These are called ghunghroos, Thara—I got them from the dance school in Chennai."

I pull the cotton ties tight and stamp my feet on the wooden floor of my room.

"What a racket!" says Nanijee.

I jump up and down, as if I'm in the practice hall.

"I love them!" I laugh, and the ghunghroos fill my bedroom with the tinkling sounds of bells.

SEASIDE CITY
The beautiful golden sands of Chennai's beach stretch all the way along the edge of the city.

CLASSICAL DANCE IS AN ANCIENT AND IMPORTANT ART FORM IN INDIA, WHICH HAS CLASSICAL MUSIC AT ITS HEART. THE DANCE ACADEMY IS IN CHENNAI, CAPITAL OF THE SOUTHERN STATE OF TAMIL NADU.

ELITE DANCERS
Dancers in India train to be accepted at the Kalakshetra Foundation. It's one of the best dance schools in the country.

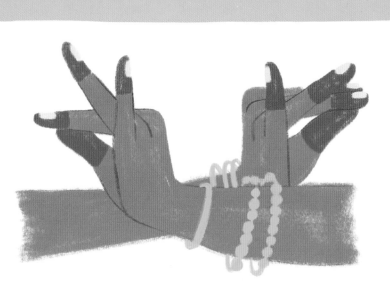

EXTREME PRECISION
Can you put your fingers and thumbs together to make an eye shape? In Bharatnatyam dance—the oldest form of classical Indian dance—dancers use their hands to make incredibly precise shapes.

40

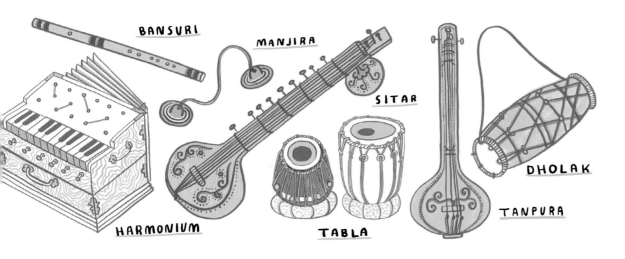

INSTRUMENTS

In addition to the jingle of the ghunghroos, the Kalakshetra dance hall is filled with the sound of stringed instruments like the sitar and tanpura, bansuri flutes, hand drums like the tabla and dholak, manjira hand cymbals, and keyboard instruments like the harmonium. The air is zinging with music.

BHARATNATYAM

Watching a performance of Bharatnatyam is like a stirring of your spirit; the jangle of bells, the music of the singers, and the extravaganza of makeup mean you won't forget it in a hurry!

A HOUSEBOAT IN KERALA

Near the bottom of the trunk, there's a photo of a boat floating on a palm-fringed blue river.

"Can you see me waving at you?" Nanijee asks as we peer at the photo together. "There were so many other boats sharing the water. Some sold fruit and vegetables, so our hosts bought everything they needed to cook up some delicious food."

"What was it like sleeping on the boat, Nanijee?"

"I loved it. The boat rocked gently, and a cool breeze floated into my cabin. And each night, the sounds of frogs and night birds sent me right off to sleep."

I lay my head in Nanijee's lap, and she sings my favorite lullaby . . . I close my eyes and imagine the waters lapping in the dark.

THE WATERS OF THE ARABIAN SEA THREAD INLAND TO FORM A SPIDERWEB OF CHANNELS ALL ALONG THE COAST OF KERALA, WHICH HOUSEBOATS NAVIGATE AT A SLOW PACE.

THE BACKWATERS

Like watery roads, the channels of Kerala can take you anywhere. And you can hop onto or off of a boat whenever you like—to visit a museum and see statues of the Buddha or to nip into a restaurant for some appam (a delicious crispy pancake served with chicken stew).

EARLY-MORNING ELEPHANTS

Kerala is full of wildlife. If you wake up at dawn, as the mists rise, you can get a ringside seat to watch wild elephants having their morning bath, showering water everywhere and trumpeting. Watch out for splashing!

THE WESTERN GHATS

A short distance inland are the famous Western Ghats—mountains that rise out of the tropical heat. There are many tea plantations, and the mountain forests are home to langur monkeys, tigers, and elephants.

SHOPPING AFLOAT

Floating shops sway along the rivers: boats piled high with bumpy green jackfruit, luscious orange papayas, and slender okra. Vendors entice shoppers by calling out their wares: "Ripe, ripe mangoes! Buy one and I'll give you two free!"

AYURVEDIC MEDICINE

Kalari Kovilakom, in the town of Kollengode, is a center for Ayurvedic medicine, an ancient way of treating health problems using fresh herbs, massage, and exercise.

SPORTS

Sports have always played an important part in Indian life. Literally digging into the past shows us that people from the very early Indus Valley civilizations rode chariots and horses, practiced archery, and put up their fists in games like boxing!

There are some ancient Indian sports that people still practice today, including kabaddi, which is a bit like tag rugby, and pehlwani, which is a type of wrestling in a dry mud arena. One of the most beautiful sports has to be kite flying, but beneath the beauty is more than a little competition. The aim of the game is to use your skill to cut your opponent's kite string and be the last kite left fluttering against the wide blue skies.

Today, India's national sport is field hockey, and both men and women compete at the international level, taking part in the Olympics. The country's Olympic team has won gold, silver, and bronze medals. But hang on: What's that huge roar? The Indian national cricket team must be nearby! It has one of the biggest followings worldwide and a very high international ranking.

HIGH ACHIEVER
Arunima Sinha is a national-level volleyball player and mountaineer born in 1989. She is the world's first female amputee to climb Mount Everest and five other world peaks, including the Vinson Massif, Antarctica's highest mountain.

PERCHED ON A POLE
The ancient gymnastic sport of mallakhamb mixes yoga with wrestling. Competitors have to balance on a carved 8½-foot (2.6-meter) wooden pole—it takes strength and confidence.

FASTBALL

Blink and you'll miss Jasprit Bumrah's cricket ball as it flies through the air— he's one of the world's top-ten fastest cricket pitchers, called bowlers.

CHAMPION BOXER

Mary Kom is an international boxing star who grew up in the eastern state of Manipur in a small village near beautiful Loktak Lake, with its blue shimmering water. She was only fifteen when she left home for the city to train, going on to win bronze at the 2012 London Olympics.

TENNIS

A trailblazer in the world of tennis, Sania Mirza is a six-time Grand Slam champion and winner of forty-three doubles titles. She is also a strong voice in encouraging girls to follow in her footsteps and take up the sport.

WOMEN IN BLUE

The Indian Women's Cricket Team is nicknamed the Women in Blue because of their team color, peacock blue. Team captain Mithali Raj is the highest scorer worldwide in women's cricket.

Karnataka

BENGALURU

"This is Nidhi Tiwari," says Nanijee, showing me a photo of a smiling woman standing in front of a khaki-green jeep. "I was lucky enough to meet her in her hometown, Bengaluru."

Nanijee tells me that Nidhi began exploring the rugged landscape of the Western Ghats when she was still young. When she later learned to drive, she would go out adventuring in her jeep—even when fierce monsoon storms lashed the roads.

When Nanijee begins to describe Nidhi's gigantic road trip, all the way from Delhi to London, I imagine it's me sitting there in the scorching driver's seat, motoring through seventeen different countries . . .

I picture myself on the starting line in Myanmar, then zooming through the mountainous eagle country of Kazakhstan . . . on to Russia and the pine forests of Europe, then finally arriving in London, ninety-seven days later: exhausted but punching the air with pride!

BENGALURU IS THE CAPITAL OF KARNATAKA STATE. AT 3,113 FEET (949 METERS) ABOVE SEA LEVEL, IT IS ONE OF THE COUNTRY'S HIGHEST CITIES—AND IS ALSO KNOWN AS THE SILICON VALLEY OF INDIA, HOUSING SOME OF THE WORLD'S BIGGEST TECH COMPANIES.

A LONG TREK
On her trip from Delhi to London, Nidhi Tiwari covered 14,800 miles (23,800 kilometers) and crossed seventeen countries!

STANDING UP FOR WOMEN

In India, women are not always viewed as having the potential to be rigorous adventurers, so Nidhi set up an organization called Women Beyond Boundaries to encourage women and girls to be adventurous—to get out into the wilderness and feel that the sky's the limit! (But then there's always space!)

FROZEN TREK

In 2016, Nidhi made "the most intense journey" of her life when she drove to Oymyakon, the coldest permanently inhabited place on earth, also known as the Pole of Cold, traveling the long, bleak Road of Bones to get to the frozen lands of Eastern Siberia.

TRADITIONAL CRAFTS

Bengaluru is famous for producing Chola statues of the Hindu god Shiva, who performs the beautiful dance of life within a circle of fire. Some of the world's most talented stonemasons and copper sculptors live in Bengaluru, passing on their skills through the generations.

Maharashtra

MUMBAI

Nanijee drapes a
turquoise outfit across
the bed: a lengha—a long
swishy skirt with sparkling
sequins carefully sewn along
the bottom—and a short blouse
embroidered with gold thread.

"It's beautiful," I say, holding the skirt
up against myself. "And just the right size."

"I guessed right, then!" Nanijee laughs as she
helps me change into it. She talks all about the Bollywood
studio tour she did in Mumbai, hoping for a glimpse of one of the
stars—and how, afterward, she bought this for me.

Nanijee switches on some music, and I whirl up and down my
room, pretending I'm in a film.

"It's such an amazing city, Thara—full of high-rise offices. But
then you can go to the beach or visit Elephanta Island by boat . . ."
She smiles. "The best bit was Amitabh Bachchan's house. He's one
of Bollywood's most famous actors. Just as I arrived, he opened the
door to his house to wave to all his fans!"

"So you got to see a star after all, Nanijee," I tell her.

ISLANDS AND BRIDGES

Mumbai is made up of seven islands, which
are, a bit like Venice, connected by bridges.
People have lived in Mumbai for a long time—
since the second century BCE.

1. MAHIM
2. WORLI
3. PAREL
4. MAZAGAON
5. BOMBAY
6. LITTLE COLABA
7. COLABA

MUMBAI IS INDIA'S LARGEST CITY
IN TERMS OF POPULATION AND
SITS ON THE WESTERN COASTLINE.
IT IS A HUGELY IMPORTANT
BUSINESS CENTER, WITH A
GLITTERING GLASS SKYLINE TO
MATCH NEW YORK'S.

CITY WILDLIFE

As well as being a city
of around 20 million,
Mumbai is home to
some incredible wildlife.
Wild leopards sneak into
the city at night and eat
scraps of food from trash
bins and alleyways.

BOLLYWOOD

The term *Bollywood* combines *Bombay* (the former name of Mumbai) and *Hollywood* (where most American movies are made). Whereas Hollywood produces about five hundred movies a year, Indian studios produce about a thousand films yearly.

WORLD-RECORD WASHING

Mumbai is home to the world's largest open-air laundry, Dhobi Ghat. It has about seven hundred washing platforms, where around two hundred families have been washing clothes for decades.

INEQUALITY

The most expensive house in the world is located in Mumbai. It's twenty-seven stories and valued at 150 billion rupees, or nearly 1.8 billion dollars. By contrast, as in many cities all over the world, millions of people in Mumbai live in poverty.

Gujarat

GIR FOREST

Nanijee brings out a leather cord necklace, strung with a sharp tooth. I hold it carefully, turning it this way and that.

"You might not believe it, Thara," says Nanijee, "but that tooth belonged to a baby lion."

"I didn't know there were lions in India," I tell her.

"There are in the forests of Gujarat," she replies. "And lion cubs are like children: when their baby teeth fall out, they get their adult teeth. The same thing will happen to you, Thara."

Nanijee places the necklace around my neck.

"Wardens collect any teeth they find—and when I went on safari, they said I could bring one home for you."

I hold the tooth and imagine my lion roaming through the thick forests, stalking its prey. The thought makes me shiver: I wouldn't want to get between the lion and its dinner—not if it has even bigger teeth as sharp as this one!

SANCTUARY
Gir National Park and Wildlife Sanctuary lies between Veraval and Junagadh, in the western state of Gujarat, and is home to the only wild Asiatic lions in the world.

NATIONAL LIONS
The Lion Capital of Ashoka, a two-thousand-year-old statue of four Asiatic lions standing back-to-back, was adopted as India's national emblem in 1950. The four lions represent power, courage, confidence, and pride.

ANCESTORS
Majestic and golden-maned, Asiatic lions are smaller than their African cousins and are the descendants of the lions that used to fight the gladiators.

GUJARAT RESTS ON THE WESTERN COAST OF INDIA, SHARING A BORDER WITH PAKISTAN IN THE NORTH, AND HAS THE COUNTRY'S LONGEST COASTLINE: 1,000 MILES (1,600 KILOMETERS).

NAWAB OF JUNAGADH

The lions were hunted for sport through history, and by the late 1800s, their numbers had dipped to only twenty—until a prince, the Nawab of Junagadh, who himself had hunted lions, decided to become their protector instead. The prince created a sanctuary for the lions on his royal lands, which is now part of Gir National Park.

Since 1989, Ahmedabad, the largest city in Gujarat, has hosted its International Kite Festival: kite makers and flyers travel from all over the world to show off their latest creations. Ahmedabad's own Rasulbhai Rahimbhai makes a regular appearance; he is known to fly five hundred kites on a single string.

Rajasthan

UDAIPUR'S LAKE PALACE

Nanijee reaches into the trunk and brings out a brightly dressed puppet. He's wearing a jeweled pink outfit with edgings of gold.

"Where did you get him from, Nanijee?" I ask, gently lifting the strings to make his arms move.

"When I was in Rajasthan, I saw this puppet dangling from a stall in the bazaar—and I knew I had to bring him home." Nanijee taps something on her phone, and a song starts to play. "Just imagine what stories he would tell us if he could speak."

Suddenly my bedroom feels like a theater, and I swoosh the puppet in time to the sitar music. He jumps and twirls, dancing around the floor, until finally the music finishes and our puppet takes a flourishing bow.

PUPPET TALES

Puppets have a long history in Rajasthan. They were used for thousands of years by royal traveling theaters to entertain and tell stories from India's famous myths and legends.

PERFECT SETTING

Visiting Udaipur—its many beautiful palaces set beside shimmering Lake Pichola, edged by the majestic purple wooded Arayalli hills—is like being in a dream.

SITUATED IN NORTHERN INDIA, RAJASTHAN IS FULL OF HISTORY. THE MAHARAJAS AND THE WARRIOR CLANS OF THE RAJPUTS HAVE LEFT BEHIND EXTRAVAGANT PALACES, BEAUTIFUL ART, AND RICH MUSICAL TRADITIONS.

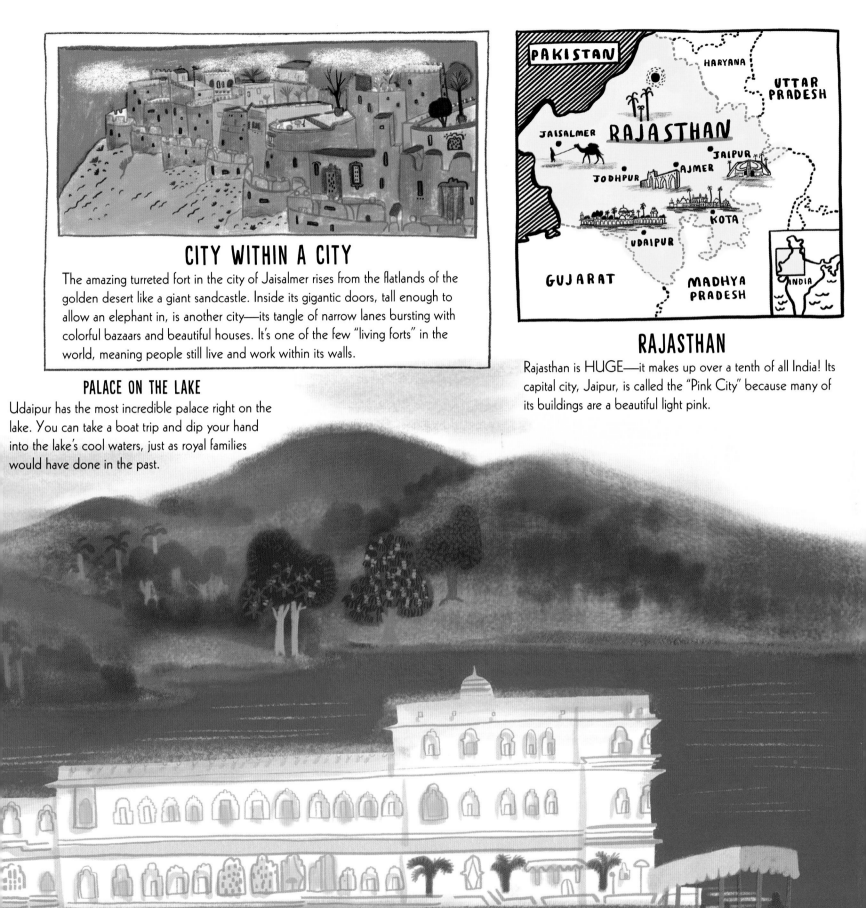

CITY WITHIN A CITY

The amazing turreted fort in the city of Jaisalmer rises from the flatlands of the golden desert like a giant sandcastle. Inside its gigantic doors, tall enough to allow an elephant in, is another city—its tangle of narrow lanes bursting with colorful bazaars and beautiful houses. It's one of the few "living forts" in the world, meaning people still live and work within its walls.

PALACE ON THE LAKE

Udaipur has the most incredible palace right on the lake. You can take a boat trip and dip your hand into the lake's cool waters, just as royal families would have done in the past.

RAJASTHAN

Rajasthan is HUGE—it makes up over a tenth of all India! Its capital city, Jaipur, is called the "Pink City" because many of its buildings are a beautiful light pink.

PAKISTAN
HARYANA
UTTAR PRADESH
JAISALMER
RAJASTHAN
JAIPUR
JODHPUR
AJMER
KOTA
UDAIPUR
GUJARAT
MADHYA PRADESH
INDIA

Punjab
GOLDEN TEMPLE

Nanijee hands me a shiny gold chain with a small painting on it.

"This is very special, Thara," she says, putting the necklace around my neck. "It's from Amritsar." Our family is Sikh, and the man in the painting is Guru Nanak, who founded our faith. "He'll always protect you," Nanijee promises.

Then she tells me all about her trip to Amritsar: about getting up early for morning prayers and sitting at the edge of the pool of holy water, called the Amrit Sarovar, with the shining golden dome of the temple reflected in the water.

"It was so peaceful and beautiful," she says, and closes her eyes.

I close my eyes too, hold my necklace, and whisper the prayer Nanijee taught me: a wish for peace across the world.

FOUNDED IN 1577 BY THE FOURTH SIKH GURU, GURU RAM DAS, AMRITSAR IS THE HOLIEST OF CITIES FOR MEMBERS OF THE SIKH FAITH. IT IS IN NORTHWEST INDIA, CLOSE TO THE BORDER WITH PAKISTAN.

WINGS OF PRAYER
Birds flutter across the wide Amrit Sarovar (whose name means "pool of nectar")—their wings sending ripples over the water like prayers before the golden dome of the temple.

SHOPPING NEAR THE SHRINE
The temple is at the heart of the city of Amritsar, and it's surrounded by a maze of streets, filled with bazaars where you can buy glittery shoes, silver wedding bangles, and all sorts of knickknacks.

TEMPLE CHORES
Everyone has to help at the temple, so no groaning allowed if you're asked to sweep the floor or do some washing up!

SIKHISM

Punjab is the home of Sikhism, founded in 1499 by Guru Nanak (the man on Thara's necklace from Nanijee). It is a faith built on equality and sharing with others. Everyone is welcome to visit Amritsar and the holiest of its holy shrines, the Harmandir Sahib or Golden Temple. Pilgrims donate money, food, and their service (called sewa) so that a meal called langar can be shared by anyone who wants it, regardless of their faith.

Sikhs wear five traditional signs of their faith. The name for each begins with a *k* in Punjabi, so they are known as the Five Ks, which are: kesh (uncut hair), kangha (comb), kara (steel bangle), kachera (white shorts, worn underneath clothing), and kirpan (symbolic dagger).

CRAFTS

Everywhere you go in India, there are markets laden with beautiful objects to buy, many of which have been handmade with love. Crafts are as important to life in India as breath, and all over the world, people treasure objects made by Indian artisans. Hand-blocked stationery, vibrant patterned rugs, and sparkling jewels are exported across the globe. Young artisans are taking ancient skills and giving them their own modern twist, selling their gorgeous pieces in shops and galleries in India's major cities and around the world through the Internet.

From weaving to embroidery, silk-spinning to cloth-printing, there are so many kinds of skillful textile art in India. Traditional clothing is very important: all over the country, women wear saris made of a length of cotton or silk about 13 to 20 feet (4 to 6 meters) long. A sari can be wrapped in countless ways, worn with a top or slip underneath. Men often wear traditional clothing such as a dhoti or lungi, as well as long buttoned shirts and loose pants called sherwanis or kurta pajamas. Men and women wear Western-style clothing, too, especially in the cities. And you'll see people wearing Nehru jackets, named for the former prime minister of India.

WEAVERS
Weaving fabrics and rugs with both traditional and modern patterns is a craft that usually takes place in people's homes and has been part of life for thousands of years. Rajasthan is home to some of the world's most skilled dhurrie weavers.

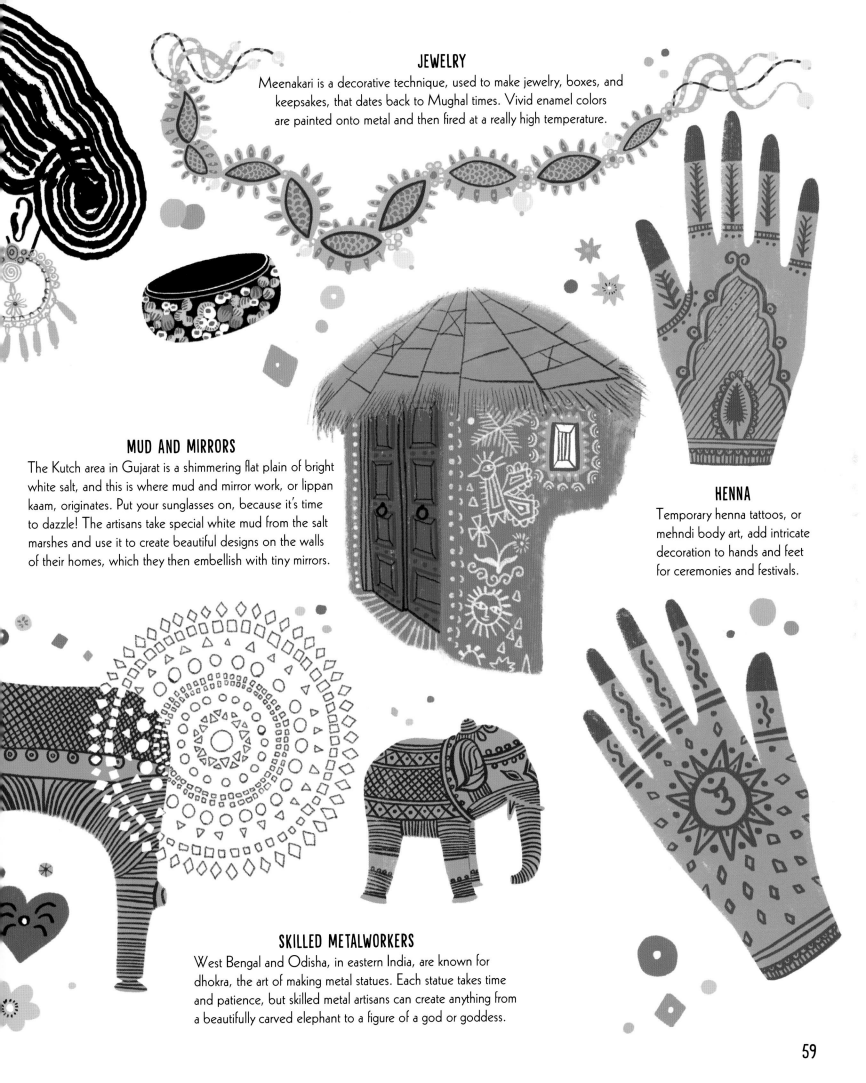

JEWELRY

Meenakari is a decorative technique, used to make jewelry, boxes, and keepsakes, that dates back to Mughal times. Vivid enamel colors are painted onto metal and then fired at a really high temperature.

MUD AND MIRRORS

The Kutch area in Gujarat is a shimmering flat plain of bright white salt, and this is where mud and mirror work, or lippan kaam, originates. Put your sunglasses on, because it's time to dazzle! The artisans take special white mud from the salt marshes and use it to create beautiful designs on the walls of their homes, which they then embellish with tiny mirrors.

HENNA

Temporary henna tattoos, or mehndi body art, add intricate decoration to hands and feet for ceremonies and festivals.

SKILLED METALWORKERS

West Bengal and Odisha, in eastern India, are known for dhokra, the art of making metal statues. Each statue takes time and patience, but skilled metal artisans can create anything from a beautifully carved elephant to a figure of a god or goddess.

Jammu and Kashmir, and Ladakh

HEMIS NATIONAL PARK

HEMIS NATIONAL PARK IS IN NORTH INDIA, IN A REGION KNOWN AS THE LAND OF HIGH PASSES, NESTLED IN THE MAGNIFICENT HIMALAYAS IN THE UNION TERRITORY OF LADAKH. THE PARK ENCOMPASSES BREATHTAKING LANDSCAPES OF WHITE-TIPPED MOUNTAINS AND SWEEPING VALLEYS FILLED WITH ICY GLACIAL WATERS.

Nanijee tells me to close my eyes, and I feel her fastening something around my neck. I open my eyes and find myself touching a small curved claw, strung onto a length of fine black string.

Nanijee tells me about the trek she took when she was a teenager and how she found the snow leopard claw hidden in the snow. The snow was deep, and she knocked a mound with her boot—and there it was, lying against the glittering ground.

I let her words carry me away until I can imagine myself there among the majestic Himalayas . . . with the deepest blue sky overhead and a single bird of prey spiraling way up high—its wings stretched wide as it hangs in the breeze.

Snow begins to fall, turning the skies silver-white, and I keep my eyes peeled for the shy, endangered snow leopard. They call it the "gray ghost" because it's an expert at hiding. Its pale, gray-dotted fur is perfectly camouflaged against the rocks.

I stay as quiet as I can and make a wish. Will I be lucky enough to spot the gray ghost?

HIDDEN IN THE HIMALAYAS

Hemis National Park is home to the endangered snow leopard. Sadly, it is estimated that there are only between 4,000 and 6,500 snow leopards left in the wild, and they're very hard to spot. But Hemis is known for its wildlife, and if you're lucky, you can spot Himalayan brown bears, double-humped Bactrian camels, and golden Eurasian lynxes with tufted ears!

CHEESEBURGER

When you get hungry in Jammu and Kashmir or Ladakh, there are so many options to choose from. For a yummy lunch you might like a kaladi kulchi. Kaladi is a kind of cheese like Halloumi or mozzarella. It's fried and stuffed into a fat bun and served like a burger.

₹7o-

KHENRAB PHUNTSOG

Growing up in the Himalayas has made Khenrab Phuntsog as nimble as a mountain goat. He's one of the park's wildlife guards and an expert at tracking snow leopards. As part of David Attenborough's team for *Planet Earth II*, he made it possible to catch snow leopard cubs on film.

WINTER

In winter you can grab your skis and zoom down the slopes in Gulmarg, where one of the world's highest cable cars will take you 12,293 feet (3,747 meters) into the mists and whirling clouds. Afterward, you can warm up with a steaming mug of Kashmiri green tea, served with strands of pale gold saffron and topped with chopped almonds. Delicious!

SUMMER

Summer in Ladakh and Jammu and Kashmir is hot! Temperatures can reach 86°F (30°C), but luckily there are lots of lakes and rivers around—if you dare to swim in their icy-cold waters! In fact, the two territories are home to at least thirty rivers that begin in the frozen landscape of the mighty Himalayas.

Punjab

VILLAGE OF THE PEACOCKS

Nanijee reaches into the trunk and brings out the last of her treasures: a shimmering blue-and-green peacock feather . . . which she tickles me with!

"Stop, Nanijee, stop!" I fall back, giggling. When I can finally catch my breath, I tell her, "I know exactly where that feather's from. It's from Moranwali, your village."

Nanijee bundles me in her arms and gives me the biggest hug.

"Well, of course," she says, smiling wide. "From one of the peacocks that like to strut along the garden walls, sweeping their long tails and showing off to everyone."

"Tell me about the animals on your farm," I ask her, even though I've heard all of the stories a hundred times before.

"Oh," says Nanijee in her best storytelling voice, "my favorites are the cows, with their huge dark eyes. When we need some milk for chai, I can crouch down and get fresh, creamy milk, straight from the udder . . ."

FERTILE FIELDS

Crops such as wheat, cotton, sugarcane, millet, and corn are grown in Punjab. On sunny days, the green-and-yellow mustard fields stretch out into the distance, sparkling against the azure-blue skies.

RAI JATS OF THALLA

Moranwali was built in 1811 by the Rai Jats of Thalla, under Maharaja Ranjit Singh—who also created the kingdom of Punjab.

At home, Punjabi families weave beautiful patterned dhurries to lay on the floor or on beds. They feature bright colors such as blues, reds, and greens and are often given as gifts.

FARAWAY FARMS

Many Punjabi families left their farms to move to the UK in the 1950s and 1960s. They always kept the farms in their hearts and saw them as second homes, often returning to renovate the farmhouses and relax in the beautiful countryside.

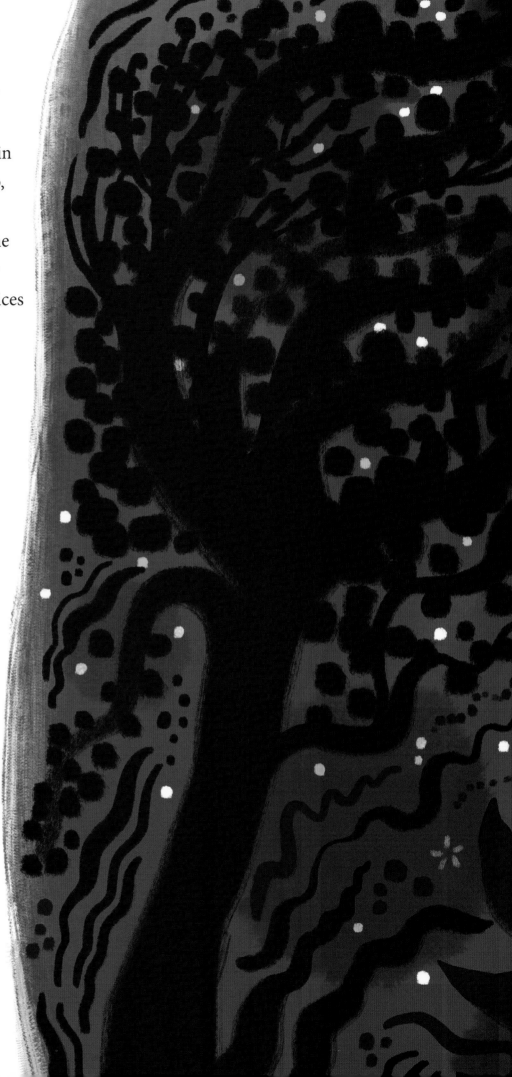

As Nanijee tucks the blanket under my chin, my mind is whirling with all the stories she's told me about growing up in India. When my eyelids begin to droop, I feel the magic taking me there.

The wind blows softly, and I smell the sweet wheat fields on the breeze; I hear the low mooing of the cows and the voices of children playing.

I join in their game of chase, and we run under the shady sheesham tree, throwing ourselves down onto the brightly colored dhurrie, where my nanijee is waiting with a cool glass of yogurt lassi.

I sip it slowly, watching the stars as they light up the night sky. I'm so relaxed, so happy here, that I can feel myself starting to drift off to sleep.

I hear Nanijee humming a lullaby and the soft click of my bedroom door. I pull the blankets tighter as her footsteps tap down the stairs. Tonight, I'll be in the village of the peacocks. Tomorrow night, who knows where Nanijee's stories will take me in India, incredible India?

THE HISTORY OF INDIA

INDIA IS AN AMAZING COUNTRY WITH A HISTORY THAT STRETCHES
FIVE THOUSAND YEARS INTO THE PAST, TO THE PREHISTORIC AGE.

10,000–8000 BCE

The oldest paintings in the rock shelters of Bhimbetka are created.

3000 BCE

The Indus Valley civilization develops in northern India and what is now Pakistan.

1700 BCE

The Indus Valley civilization collapses, and Aryan peoples arrive from Central Asia.

1221–1400 CE

Genghis Khan leads the first Mongol invasion of India; a later Mongol invasion is mounted by Timur in 1398.

1000–1210 CE

The Ghaznavid dynasty invades from the north; the Delhi Sultanate is founded in 1210.

1498 CE

Portuguese explorer Vasco da Gama establishes trade between Europe and India.

1526 CE

The Mughal Empire is established by Babur.

1556 CE

Akbar the Great becomes the third Mughal emperor.

1920 CE

Mahatma Gandhi begins a campaign of nonviolence against the British government.

1911 CE

The British government moves the capital from Calcutta to Delhi.

1885 CE

The Indian National Congress is formed in an effort to gain independence for India.

500 BCE

Siddhartha Gautama founds Buddhism.

327 BCE

Alexander the Great arrives in India.

321–185 BCE

Rule of the Mauryan Empire

712 CE

Islam arrives in India.

320–550 CE

Rule of the Gupta Empire, during which time the decimal numeral system is invented

100 BCE– 203 CE

Rule of the Satavahana dynasty; in 60 CE, the Kushan Empire takes control of northern India.

1600 CE

The British East India Company is founded in Britain and begins trade in India.

1632– 1653 CE

Mughal emperor Shah Jahan builds the Taj Mahal.

1858 CE

The British East India Company is abolished and the British Empire takes full rule of India.

1857 CE

Indian troops rebel against the rule of the British East India Company.

1757 CE

The British East India Company defeats the rulers of Bengal at the Battle of Plassey and gains political power.

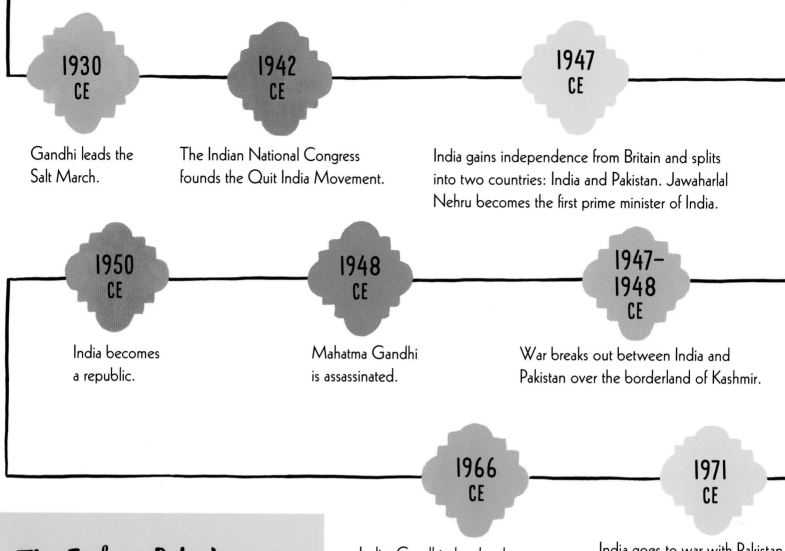

1930 CE

Gandhi leads the Salt March.

1942 CE

The Indian National Congress founds the Quit India Movement.

1947 CE

India gains independence from Britain and splits into two countries: India and Pakistan. Jawaharlal Nehru becomes the first prime minister of India.

1950 CE

India becomes a republic.

1948 CE

Mahatma Gandhi is assassinated.

1947–1948 CE

War breaks out between India and Pakistan over the borderland of Kashmir.

1966 CE

Indira Gandhi, the daughter of Jawaharlal Nehru, is elected prime minister.

1971 CE

India goes to war with Pakistan over the creation of the country of Bangladesh from East Pakistan.

The Indian-Pakistan Border at Attari-Wagah

Every day since 1959, at the border between Attari, India, and Wagah, Pakistan, military guards of both countries have performed a border ceremony in which the flags of each country are lowered together.

Each side is dressed in military uniforms—bright red and khaki for India and dark green for Pakistan. Both sides sport special crested headgear as well.

During the ceremony, the guards kick their legs high in the air and march up and down the border crossing before lowering the flags of each country. Thousands of tourists come from all over to see this performance, and they hoot and cheer throughout.

This dance-like performance is exciting to see and is regarded as a symbol of cooperation between the two countries.

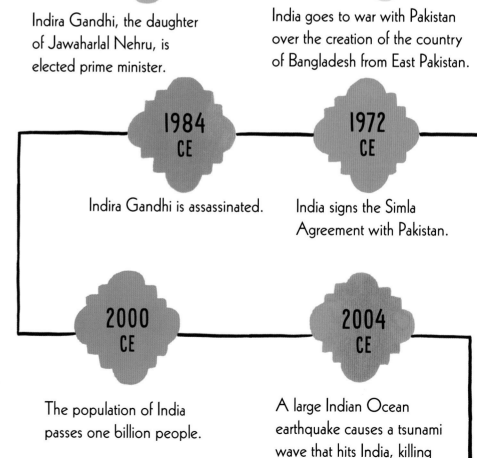

1984 CE

Indira Gandhi is assassinated.

1972 CE

India signs the Simla Agreement with Pakistan.

2000 CE

The population of India passes one billion people.

2004 CE

A large Indian Ocean earthquake causes a tsunami wave that hits India, killing more than 10,000 people.

Father of the Nation
Mohandas Karamchand Gandhi

In 1869, beside the turquoise-blue Arabian Sea in Porbandar, Gujarat, a very important person was born: Mohandas Karamchand Gandhi. When he was little, his family loved him and called him "Manu." No one could have foreseen that he would go on to become known as the father of the nation or given the name Mahatma, meaning saint.

How do you feel when things are unfair? Gandhi lived during the time when India was ruled by the British, and there was a lot of unfairness and inequality. He was a person who had strong ideas about right and wrong and always fought for everyone to be equal. He was a very determined person, and through hard work, he went to London to study law, then worked as a lawyer in South Africa.

At the time in South Africa, the government treated white people as though they were better than people of color. Gandhi was once asked to get off a bus because he was not white. This made him angry and sad at the same time and gave him a passion for standing up for people's rights. One of the most remarkable things about Gandhi is that he believed strongly in peace: he organized strikes, nonviolent protests, and fasts to help improve working conditions. And he used this way of thinking to achieve independence for India from British rule in 1947.

One of his most famous protests was the Salt March. The British government made a law to force people to buy expensive imported British salt, even though there was plenty of salt in India. Joined by thousands of people, Gandhi led a twenty-four-day walk to the coast, where they collected salt from the sea.

Gandhi was, and is, adored by people all over India—and around the world. He influenced many leaders, including Martin Luther King Jr. and the Dalai Lama, and was nominated for the Nobel Peace Prize five times.

The Indian Flag

The Indian flag was designed and fluttered high for the first time in 1947, for Indian Independence. Glowing saffron orange stands for objectivity, white for truth and peace, and forest green for abundance. At its center sits the twenty-four-spoke Ashoka Chakra.

The flag represents freedom; the belief that everyone is equal, regardless of class, race, or gender; and the idea that the country should welcome change, like the wheel that keeps turning.

 # Index

Find Out More

More facts and figures: **www.britannica.com/facts/India**

More about Indian languages: **https://utalk.com/news/how-many-languages-are-there-in-india/**

More about Indian music: **https://indianmusicexperience.org/blogs/the-evolution-of-indian-music/**

More about Indian history: **www.dkfindout.com/uk/history/modern-india/**

More about Indian wildlife: **www.wwfindia.org/** and the David Attenborough documentary series *Secrets of Wild India* (National Geographic, 2012)

And for stories set in or inspired by India: **www.booksfortopics.com/booklist-india** and **https://booktrust.org.uk/news-and-features/features/2020/september/9-brilliant-childrens-books -inspired-by-india-chosen-by-jasbinder-bilan/**

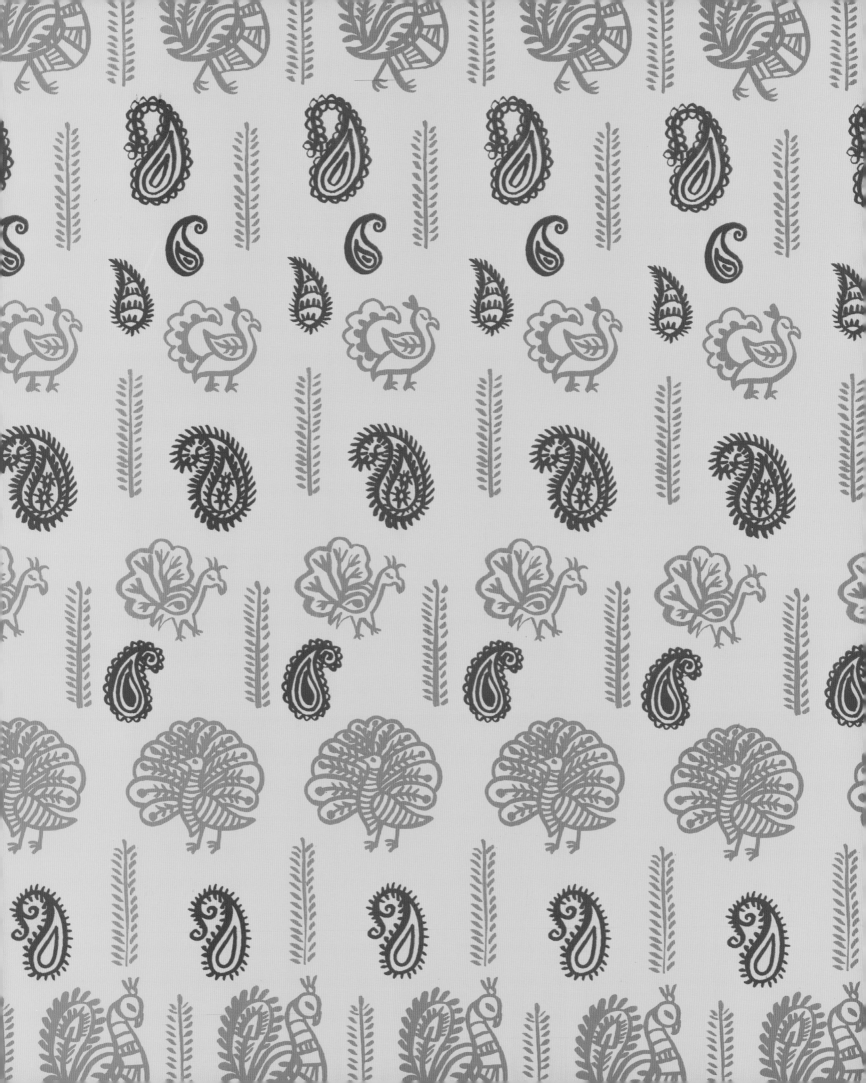